All I Want for Christmas

Opening the Gifts of God's Grace

James W. Moore

All I Want
for Christmas

Opening the Gifts of God's Grace

ALL I WANT FOR CHRISTMAS
Copyright © 2016 by Abingdon Press
All rights reserved.

Scripture quotations unless noted otherwise are from the Common English Bible. Copyright © 2011 by the Common English Bible. All rights reserved. Used by permission. *www.CommonEnglishBible.com.*

Scripture quotations marked (NRSV) are taken from the New Revised Standard Version of the Bible, copyright 1989, Division of Christian Education of the National Council of the Churches of Christ in the United States of America. Used by permission. All rights reserved.

ISBN: 9781501824197

16 17 18 19 20 21 22 23 24 25—10 9 8 7 6 5 4 3 2 1
MANUFACTURED IN THE UNITED STATES OF AMERICA

Contents

Introduction

From the time the wise men came to Jesus bringing gifts, Christmas has been a time of giving. . .

—gifts to our loved ones,

—gifts to the less fortunate,

—gifts to the church,

—gifts to favorite charities,

—gifts to family,

—gifts to friends,

—and even gifts to our pets.

In the best spirit of Christmas, we give and receive Christmas gifts, remembering the greatest Christmas gift of all: God's gift of the Christ Child, God's gift to us of a Savior!

As we give and receive Christmas gifts, it is incredibly important to remember that the best Christmas gifts are wrapped in heaven. Unfortunately, sometimes we concentrate so much on the gifts we want to give to each other and receive from each other (nice as that practice is) that we miss the special gifts Christmas has for us.

As you're going to discover in this book, Christmas has some amazing gifts for us. But the truth is that we need the miracle of God's grace to see them, feel them, hear them, wrap our arms around them, and celebrate them. In thinking of this recently, I began to think through this very personal question: What are the gifts I would really like to receive from Christmas this year? And that is what this book is all about: our thoughts and ruminations about the amazing, life-changing gifts Christmas has for us.

—*Jim Moore*

1. The Gift of Good News
Matthew 1:18-25

Christmas Has Some Special Gifts for Us

Have you heard about the college football coach who was having a tough time on a Saturday afternoon? His team was up against their long-time archrival, and they were playing for the league championship. Injuries were taking their toll, which was making the coach more and more upset. In the first half, his first-string quarterback got hurt. Early in the second half, his second-string quarterback went down and had to be carried off the field. Then in the last quarter, his third-string quarterback was knocked out. There were two minutes left in the game, and the score was tied 14 to 14. With no other options left at quarterback, the coach called for McTavish. Now, McTavish was a freshman, the fourth-string quarterback . . . and the team's punter: When McTavish ran up to the coach to be put into the game, this is the conversation that took place:

COACH: "McTavish, are you listening to me?"

McTAVISH: "Yes, sir."

COACH: "Can you follow my instructions?"

McTAVISH: "Yes, sir!"

COACH: "Can you do *exactly* what I tell you to do?"

McTAVISH: "Yes, sir!"

COACH: "OK. . . . Listen closely. There are two minutes left in the game, the score is tied 14 to 14, and we have the ball on our own ten yard line. There's no way we can win, so we are going to settle for a tie. In order to do that, we need to try to run as much time off the clock as we can. Now here's what I want you to do. Get in there and follow my plan exactly, or you'll never play for this team again. Don't think. Just follow this plan:

On the first play, run a quarterback sneak. On the second play, run a quarterback sneak. On the third play, run a quarterback sneak. And then on the fourth play, you drop back and punt the ball out of the stadium; kick it as far as you can!"

With those instructions, McTavish took the field. On the first play, he ran the quarterback sneak just as his coach had instructed him. And believe it or not, the line opened up, and he ran straight up the field for a thirty-yard gain! On the second play, the same thing happened. He ran the quarterback sneak and again, amazingly, he gained thirty yards. On the third play, McTavish ran the quarterback sneak again. Incredibly, once more there was a big hole in the center of the line. He dashed through it and then cut to the outside and he went twenty-nine yards. A defender knocked him out of bounds just inches short of the goal line, inches short of the winning touchdown. Then on the fourth play, McTavish dropped back—and punted the ball out of the stadium! The gun sounded ending the game.

The crowd could not believe what they had just seen. The coach threw down his hat in disgust and stomped it. And then he ran onto the field in search of McTavish.

"McTavish!" the coach shouted. "What in the world were you doing?"

"Just what you told me to do," the young quarterback answered.
"Oh, no," said the coach. "What on earth were you *thinking*?"

McTavish answered, "I was thinking that we have got to have the dumbest coach in America."

McTavish's problem was that he had a closed mind. He was so focused on following the coach's instructions to the letter that he lost sight of the big picture of the football game and the incredible chance he had to win it. Sometimes that is precisely our problem at Christmas. We get so caught up in the hectic excitement and busyness of the season that we close our minds to the real truth of Christmas. We concentrate so much on the gifts we want to give each other and receive from each other that we miss the special gifts Christmas has for us. Christmas has some wonderful gifts for us.

The first Christmas gift I want to share with you is the gift of good news. Christmas gives us the gift of good news of Jesus' birth, the good news that God is with us! This gift of good news truly is a gift that keeps on giving, because it inspires our faith, grounds our hope, and leads us to love. Through the good news of Jesus, Christmas gives us the gifts of faith, and hope, and love. I'm sure you will think of others as well.

Christmas Gives Us the Gift of Faith

At Christmas, our faith gets a shot in the arm. At Christmas, we renew our faith by remembering afresh the real priorities of life. A few years ago, one of our missionaries in Kenya was given a Jeep to help him in his missionary rounds. He used the Jeep as he went from village to village to preach, to teach the Scriptures, and to help the people. However, after he had the Jeep for a few months, all of a sudden it refused to start. He looked under the hood, but not knowing anything about automobile engines, he just presumed the battery was worn out. He found that he could get the Jeep started by getting some folks to give him a push. Or he could park it headed down a hill and roll it off, engaging the clutch. For two years, the missionary started the Jeep like that. When time came for his furlough, his replacement arrived and the missionary showed his replacement how to start the Jeep by pushing it off or rolling it down a hill. The new missionary looked under the hood for a moment and then he said: "Doctor, I think I see the problem: The battery cable has come loose from the starter." The new missionary reached in, reconnected the loose cable, got in the driver's seat, turned the key—and the engine roared to life.

In like manner, Christmas reconnects us to our power source. As we look forward to the birth of Jesus, we feel God come close and recognize that nothing else can fulfill our longing for a better world. The reminder of God's presence ignites our faith and reinvigorates our life in Christ. One key word, more than any other, captures how Christmas reconnects us and inspires faith. Found in the Scripture lesson in Matthew 1, the word is *Emmanuel*. When the angel appears to Joseph and tells him about Mary's pregnancy and Jesus' conception by the Holy Spirit (Matthew 1:18-21), the Scripture tells us that this happened to fulfill the words of "the prophet," meaning Isaiah (verse 22). "Look!" the author writes in verse 23, "A virgin will become pregnant and give birth to a son,

> And they will call him Emmanuel."

Emmanuel means God with us. The Christmas gift of good news is the knowledge and assurance that God is with us! Christ came to underscore this good, joyful news that God is with us . . . and nothing can separate us from God. Did you catch that? Nothing can separate us from God's love and care. Not even death! If that doesn't inspire faith, I don't know what would. That is God's promise. That is the message, the good news, of Christmas. "Emmanuel" . . . God is with us! That is our faith. What a fantastic and amazing Christmas gift that is!

Christmas Gives Us the Gift of Hope

For many years, the poem "Footprints in the Sand" has been well known and much beloved. It's usually attributed to an unknown author, though several people have claimed to have written it. It's readily found in books, posters, or other written works meant to comfort and inspire. Sometimes when I feel down, or a little blue, or just need some reassurance, I go back and read it again. It restores my strength and gives me confident hope.

Do you know the poem? It describes a dream in which someone walked on a beach talking with God, who walked alongside the dreamer. The dreamer sees visions of her life in the sky, always with two sets of footprints symbolizing how God has walked with her. She notices, however, that during the most difficult times of life, there is only one set of footprints. She asks God why he left her alone during the bad times, when she needed him the most. God replies that he did not leave her . . . there is only one set of footprints during those times because that is when God carried her.

This is the message of Christmas, isn't it? Even during life's worst times, when we think we are alone, God is with us. And that gives us a powerful hope that strengthens us no matter what happens. Again, the word is "Emmanuel." God realizes that we need help, and God sends us a Savior. And in so doing God gives us hope.

Many years ago, a submarine sank, powerless, off the New England coast. Ships were rushed to the scene, and divers went down to see if anything could be done. The crew members in the submarine clung desperately to life as their oxygen supply was slowly exhausted. The divers communicated with the crew members inside the sub by tapping out the dots and dashes of Morse code. Time was running out, and after a long pause a question was slowly tapped out from inside the submarine: "Is.......there.......any.......hope?"

The answer of Christmas is a resounding "Yes!" because God is with us. That is the gift of good news that stands at the foundation of our hope. God will not desert us. In the gift of good news, Christmas gives us Faith and Hope.

Christmas Gives Us the Gift of Love

The good news of Emmanuel inspires faith, and hope . . . and above all, love. God comes to be with us for the simple reason that God loves us. God sends Jesus to save his people from their sins (Matthew 1:21) because God loves us. And in being with us, God shows us the way of love so that we might love others. Faith, hope, and love all remain, writes Paul in 1 Corinthians 13:13. "And the greatest of these is love."

In his book *Who Switched the Price Tags* (Royal Publishers, 1986), Tony Campolo tells a beautiful story about a schoolteacher named Miss Thompson, which underscores the power of love (pages 69–72). Miss Thompson was a conscientious fifth-grade teacher who tried to treat all her students the same. But there was one little boy who was impossible, and it was very difficult for her even to like him. His name was Teddy Stallard. Teddy didn't seem to be interested in school. His schoolwork was horrendous, and his attitude was even worse. He was so difficult that Miss Thompson became very resentful of him. She disliked him so much that she almost enjoyed giving him Fs.

Then Christmas time came, and the boys and girls in Miss Thompson's room brought her some gifts. Teddy brought her a crudely wrapped present, a brown crushed paper sack with an old, frayed red ribbon around it. Inside Miss Thompson discovered a gaudy rhinestone bracelet with half the stones missing and a half-full bottle of perfume. The children began to smirk and giggle at the simple gifts. But the spirit of Christmas, the spirit of love, bubbled up in Miss Thompson. She put the bracelet on and opened the perfume. She dabbed some on her wrist and invited the children to smell. "Isn't this bracelet beautiful?" she asked the children. "Doesn't this perfume smell lovely?" Taking their cue from her, the children responded with "oohs" and "aahs."

At the end of school, little Teddy came to Miss Thompson's desk and said: "Miss Thompson, Miss Thompson . . . you smell just like my mother used to smell . . . and her bracelet looks real pretty on you too. I'm glad you liked my presents." As they talked, Miss Thompson learned that Teddy's mother had died when he was in second grade and that this father, unable to cope, had turned to alcohol. Miss Thompson's heart went out to little Teddy. She saw him in a new light, and for the first time she saw him with the eyes of love.

When Teddy left, Miss Thompson said a prayer. She asked God for forgiveness for the attitude she had held toward Teddy. To make a long story short, from that day forward Miss Thompson became a new teacher, and Teddy became a new student. Both Teddy's attitude and his grades dramatically improved.

Teddy kept up with Miss Thompson through the years, and he eventually became a doctor. Some years later, Miss Thompson received a letter from Teddy asking if she'd come to his wedding and sit in his mother's place of honor. "You are all the family I have left now," he said.

That moment of Christmas love, many years before, had been good news for Teddy Stallard. It changed his life. It turns out it was also a gift of good news for Miss Thompson, because it changed her life too!

Emmanuel, God with us, is the Christmas gift of good news. And this gift of good news inspires our faith, nurtures our hope, and empowers us to love. In a very special way, faith, hope, and love come down at Christmas!

Questions for Reflection and Discussion

1. How did Joseph react when he first heard the news of Mary's pregnancy? How hard do you think it was for him eventually to receive this message as "good news"?

2. Describe a time in your life when you have felt especially close to God, as if God were very near to you. How does the memory of that moment inspire faith or hope for you?

3. Where do you see faith, hope, and love in the account of Mary's pregnancy and Jesus' birth in Matthew 1:18-25? What is the relationship between these three virtues in that story?

4. At the beginning of this season of Advent, what reasons do you see for hope in your life or in our world? How do these circumstances point to the presence of God with us?

5. Does it require faith to recognize these reasons for hope? Why, or why not?

6. Where do you see evidence of God's love for you? How can you show someone else that God loves them?

Prayer

God, you are with us. May this word from you give us reassurance and hope for the presence and the future. Give us eyes to see you and ears to hear you. And give us hearts to receive the good news of Emmanuel. Grant us faith, hope, and love that are grounded in your presence. In Jesus' name we pray. Amen.

Focus for the Week

God is with us. God is with you. This week, pay close attention to God's presence. Spend some purposeful, set-apart time with God in prayer or in Scripture reading, reminding yourself that God is always near. Look for ways to recognize the presence of God in silence, in nature, in other people, and in the circumstances of your life. Give thanks to God for the faith, hope, and love that God's presence inspires.

Daily Devotions

Read the Scriptures for the daily devotions and reflect on what they say to you about the gift of good news. Record your insights in the space provided, using the questions at the top of each page as a guide.

Day 1

Isaiah 52:1-12

A Message of Good News

"How beautiful upon the mountains are the feet of a messenger who proclaims peace, who brings good news!" (Isaiah 52:7). The author of Isaiah 52 speaks a message of good news to the people of Judah. Many years before, their holy city of Jerusalem had been conquered and they had been sent into exile in Babylon. But now, Isaiah says, God has redeemed them and will bring them back home. To the people living in exile, this message of God's redemption was surely good news that they received with joy and gratitude.

This good news is grounded in God's strength and love for the people. God rules, and the whole world has witnessed the victory of the Lord. This victory is made known in the redemption of God's people and their return to their ancestral land. They can rest assured that God goes before them to lead the way and behind them to keep them safe. It is the prophet's joy and blessing to be the one who proclaims this good news to God's people.

What message of good news do you and the people around you need to hear?

How does God's love and strength bring a message of hope into your world? How is God calling you to bear this good news?

Day 2

Isaiah 7:1-17

God With Us

"The young woman is pregnant and is about to give birth to a son, and she will name him Immanuel" (Isaiah 7:14). The Gospel of Matthew tells us that this word from Isaiah is fulfilled in the birth of Jesus: The virgin Mary is the "young woman," and Jesus is the son called Emmanuel, which means "God with us" (Matthew 1:22-23). But in Isaiah's own day, the prophet spoke these words with a different situation in mind. The kingdom of Judah was under attack from two kings, Rezin of Aram and Pekah of Israel, and the people of Judah and Jerusalem were terrified (Isaiah 7:1-2). Their hearts "shook as the trees of a forest shake when there is a wind" (Isaiah 7:2). But in the midst of this threat and resulting fear, Isaiah offers a profound word of hope to Judah's king. "Don't fear, and don't lose heart," Isaiah says (Isaiah 7:4). God is with the people of Judah, and the birth of Immanuel is a sign of God's presence and protection.

God's people can trust in God's presence and protection. No matter what happens, God is with us and we need not be afraid.

What sign of God's presence and protection do you see around you? How do you experience the promise of "God with us" during this Advent season?

How will trust in God's presence shape your life in the days and weeks ahead?

Day 3

Hebrews 11:1-40

The Faith of the Faithful

"Faith is the reality of what we hope for, the proof of what we don't see. The elders in the past were approved because they showed faith" (Hebrews 11:1-2). Faith is a gift that we receive anew during Advent and Christmas. And we are not alone in receiving it. The author of Hebrews recalls the great history of God's people, naming many of our spiritual ancestors and reminding us how they lived by faith. From Abel through David, Samuel, and the prophets, faith characterized their lives. And we who know Christ have received the promise for which they hoped in faith. In Hebrews Chapter 12, the author calls these people "a great cloud of witnesses surrounding us" (12:1). The witness of their faith is an example to encourage and challenge us to have faith of our own.

With the coming birth of Christ and the knowledge that God is with us, our faith is strengthened. We too can live by faith, the reality of what we hope for. In doing so we join that great cloud of witnesses, communicating to ourselves and to others that God is at work in our lives and in our world.

Who has been a powerful example of faith for you? How does that person's life exemplify faith in God?

What legacy of faith will you leave to those who come after you?

Day 4

Romans 8:18-39

We Were Saved in Hope

"I'm convinced that nothing can separate us from God's love in Christ Jesus our Lord: not death or life, not angels or rulers, not present things or future things, not powers or height or depth, or any other thing that is created" (Romans 8:38-39). In this section of Paul's Letter to the Romans, he contrasts present suffering with the glory for which he and his fellow Christians hope. Though bad things can happen and seem powerful, God's love is more powerful still. Paul's words challenge us to see hardship as a part of a larger story of God delivering the whole world, reminding us that God is on our side. We can have hope, and the Holy Spirit will sustain us.

Advent likewise calls us to a posture of hope as we look forward to the birth of Christ. We remember in this season of the year that our hopes have not yet been fulfilled. . . . Christ has been born, but we wait for Christ to come again to finish the work of new creation. In the meantime, we are nevertheless hopeful, because "if God is for us, who is against us?" (Romans 8:31).

What circumstances cause you to have little hope or to doubt God's presence?

How does the Holy Spirit sustain you even when you don't know what to pray?

Day 5

1 Corinthians 13:1-13

The Greatest of These Is Love

"If I speak in tongues of human beings and of angels but I don't have love, I'm a clanging gong or a clashing cymbal" (1 Corinthians 13:1). A well-known quotation in sports, attributed to UCLA football coach Red Sanders, says, "Winning isn't everything. . . . It's the only thing!" The apostle Paul seems to have the same attitude toward the Christian virtue of love. One might be the most faithful, generous, knowledgeable, patient person alive, but without love it's all useless. In other words, love isn't everything. . . . It's the only thing!

When we read Paul's meditation on love in 1 Corinthians 13, we sense that Paul feels he can't overstate the importance of love. Knowledge and prophecy will come to an end, but love will never come to an end. It's not that knowledge, prophecy, and other spiritual gifts are unimportant. It's just that love is so much more important that everything else pales in comparison. Paul encourages us to pursue love above all else, loving one another as God has loved us.

When have you witnessed the power of love?

How does the love of God revealed through Christ's birth inspire you to love others?

Day 6

Matthew 28:16-20

Therefore Go

"Look, I myself will be with you every day until the end of this present age" (Matthew 28:20). Jesus' promise to his disciples at the end of the Gospel of Matthew echoes the hope expressed at Jesus' birth. When he is born, Jesus is called Emmanuel, meaning "God with us" (Matthew 1:22-23). Now after the Resurrection, Jesus reminds the disciples that he will always be with them. So Matthew begins and ends with the assurance that God is with us in the person of Jesus Christ.

This assurance grounds Jesus' instructions to his followers to go and make disciples of all nations, baptizing them and teaching them to obey Jesus' words. Christmas gives to us the gift of good news, which grounds our faith, hope, and love. It's our calling as Jesus' followers to tell this good news to others. It's not something most of us are comfortable doing. The task can be risky and challenging. But we can do it boldly, because Christ is with us!

How did you first hear the good news of Jesus?

Who in your life or community needs to hear the good news? How will you share it with them?

2. The Gift of a New Understanding

Luke 1:39-56

The Christmas Gifts That Are Just Heavenly

There is an old story about a factory that was having a terrible problem with employee theft. Valuable items were being stolen every day, and the factory managers simply could not figure out who was doing it or how it was being done. They just knew that they were suffering significant financial losses due to the persistent stealing, and they knew that it was an inside job.

So they hired a security firm to search literally every employee as he or she left at the end of the day. Most of the workers willingly went along with emptying their pockets and having their lunch boxes checked, because they were made to realize how serious the "theft problem" had become. It became a routine, and the employees and security agents soon came to go through the drill quickly as a part of the day's work.

But one man would go through the gate every day at closing time with a wheelbarrow full of trash, which always slowed things down. The exasperated security guard would have to spend a half-hour or more digging through the food wrappers, the aluminum cans, and the Styrofoam cups to see if any valuables were being smuggled out. He never found anything! Weeks and weeks went by and he never found anything, but still great losses were being suffered due to employee theft.

Finally one day, the guard could no longer stand it. He said to the man, "Look, I know you're up to something, but I can't figure it out. Every day I check every last bit of trash in the wheelbarrow, and I never find anything worth stealing. It's driving me crazy. Tell me what you're up to and I promise not to report you. The man shrugged and said, "It's simple. I'm stealing wheelbarrows!"

Sometimes we can't see the forest for the trees. Sometimes we can't see the wheelbarrow for the trash. And sometimes we can't see the gifts Christmas gives to us because we're too busy focusing on the distractions as if they are the truly important details.

Christmas is a time for giving. We all know that's true because even now we are all involved in "making our lists and checking 'em twice." But here in this chapter, I want to turn the coin over, go a step deeper, and take a look with you at a few more of the gifts Christmas gives to us. Yes, the gifts Christmas gives to us. They are, in the end, the most important gifts of all. These are the Christmas gifts that are just heavenly.

Some years ago, our family was invited to a unique birthday party. A close friend asked us to come to his home to celebrate his wife's birthday. Ten or twelve people attended the party, and we were all told rather strongly not to bring gifts. "NO GIFTS PLEASE!" the invitation said in bold, capital letters with two exclamation points. The guest of honor didn't want any gifts, and she really meant it. We had a delightful evening: a sumptuous meal, excellent entertainment, delightful conversation, good fun, and fellowship. Finally, the cake was brought in and we all sang "Happy Birthday."

But then something happened at this birthday party that I had never seen before. The man stood up and with a wide smile, he said: "My wife, Diana, celebrates her birthday in a unique way. Instead of receiving gifts from others, she likes to celebrate her birthday by giving gifts to those she loves." Diana then proceeded to bring out special gifts for all the people there.

Something like this happens at Christmas. The Christ Child celebrates his birthday by giving special gifts to those he loves. This means that Christmas has some very special gifts for you and me! One such gift is the gift of a new understanding, a new way of seeing ourselves and the world around us. Remember how it's expressed in Mary's song of praise: "The mighty one has done great things for me" (Luke 1:49). God, the Mighty One, does great things for us by giving us a new understanding. Let me list for your consideration three ways that we receive a new understanding that Christmas gives to us. Christmas gives to us:

(1) A new picture of God
(2) A new partnership with others
(3) A new purpose for living

Now, let's take a look at these.

Christmas Gives Us a New Picture of God

First, Christmas gives us a new picture of God, a fresh new understanding of what God is like.

You see, this is the good news of Christmas: Jesus comes to show us what God is really like, and the picture he paints is the portrait of love. Before Jesus came, many people had only vague and shadowy—and often quite wrong—ideas about God. God was sometimes depicted as harsh, hostile, vengeful, or vindictive. But Jesus came to show us that God is love!

When I was about nine years old and living in Memphis, there was an older man in our neighborhood named Toby. He was an Italian farmer with long gray hair and a shaggy beard. He wore the clothes of a hard-working farmer: dirty overalls, dusty boots, and a gray sweat-stained hat. We even though his face looked like leather. He lived alone; he was the closest thing to a hermit I ever knew. He had very little social contact, but he did buy his groceries at the little neighborhood grocery store that our family owned and ran.

My brother Bob was eleven years old; my sister, Susie, was three; and I was nine—and we were scared to death of Mr. Toby. It was said that Mr. Toby didn't like children, and he didn't look like he would like them, and we weren't about to ask him. To us he was scary, and we steered clear of him. As a matter of fact, every time Mr. Toby came around, the three of us (my brother, sister, and I) would run and hide behind the hedge, and there we would wait in silence, shaking with fear until Mr. Toby was gone out of sight again. We were so afraid of him that we actually had nightmares about him.

But then one day, we came to see Mr. Toby in a new light. We were playing in the yard when our pet cat was hit by a car. The cat came limping into the yard dragging his back right leg. It was fractured. The three of us children were on our knees over the cat, crying and rubbing our pet. We were so upset that we didn't hear someone walk up. Suddenly, our eyes fell on two dusty boots. We looked up to see the crusty old face of Mr. Toby.

Mr. Toby had a look of compassion in his eyes. He dropped to his knees and very tenderly gathered our injured cat up into his arms, and lovingly began to pet him. Then, quick as a flash, he began barking out orders: "Susie, go get a towel! Bob, you get some tape! And Jim, you go in the store and bring me two Popsicle sticks!" When we returned with the supplies he had requested, Mr. Toby was holding the cat in his arms, rocking him like a baby, and singing a soothing lullaby to him. A trace of tears had streamed down into his beard.

He made a nice, neat splint for the cat's leg, then covered him with the towel and took him in the house and laid him in his bed. Then he went into the store and came back with three pieces of bubble gum. As he gave us the gum, he said: "I know about animals. Don't you kids worry now, your cat is going to be all right." Then with a smile and a wink, he turned and walked away.

Do you know what? After that day we weren't ever afraid of Mr. Toby again. We didn't hide from him anymore. In fact, we became great friends. We had a whole new perception of him, a new picture that fed into a new relationship. This new picture was not a portrait of fear, but now one of love and appreciation. That experience helped us children to see Mr. Toby as he really was, and we loved him from that day on.

This may well be the best gift Christmas gives to us: a new picture of God, a new understanding of what God is really like.

Christmas gives us a new experience of God's compassion and tenderness, out of which we can form a new relationship with God, built not on fear, but love!

Christmas Gives Us a New View of Others

Christmas gives us not only a new understanding of God, but also a new way of understanding other people. The gift of Christmas involves a new respect, a new regard for other people. Christmas shows us that people are more important than things; they are not pawns to be used, but persons to be loved. Also, Christmas shows us that the best way to love God is to love God's children.

What better way to express this than with the powerful Christmas story entitled "The Story of the Other Wise Man," which was written in 1895 by Henry Van Dyke and has been reprinted and retold many times since then. This story tells of a fourth wise man called Artaban. He, too, set out to follow the star along with the three wise men of Christmas tradition. He took with him three gifts: a sapphire, a ruby, and a pearl. Three priceless gifts for the newborn king. Artaban was riding hard to meet his three friends at the place they had agreed upon. The time was short. The other three wise men would leave if he were late.

Suddenly, Artaban saw a dim figure on the ground before him. It was a traveler stricken with fever and dying. What should Artaban do? If he stayed to help, he would surely miss his friends and they would go on without him. But could he really leave this man who was suffering? Artaban decided to stay and help the sick man. But he missed the caravan, and the other wise men left without him. Now he was alone. He needed camels and bearers to help him across the desert, because he did not have the supplies to do it by himself. So, he had to sell his sapphire to purchase what he needed. Artaban was sad because the King of kings would never receive the sapphire.

He journeyed on and in due time came to Bethlehem, but again, he was too late. Joseph, Mary, and the baby had fled to Egypt to escape the devious plot of Herod to kill all the children of the town under two years old. Artaban was in a house in Bethlehem where there was a little child. Soldiers came to the door, and the weeping of stricken mothers could be heard across the darkness. Artaban stood tall and powerful in the doorway, with the ruby in his hand. He bribed the captain not to enter the house. The child was saved, and the mother was overjoyed. But now the ruby was gone, and Artaban was sad because the King of kings would never receive his ruby.

Artaban continued his quest with his last gift, a pearl of great price. For years and years he wandered, looking in vain for the King of kings. More than thirty years passed, and eventually Artaban came to Jerusalem. A crucifixion was about to take place. When Artaban heard about this Jesus of Nazareth who was to be crucified, the fourth wise man instinctively recognized that this was the one he'd been looking for. Jesus was the King he had been seeking over all those years.

Artaban hurried toward Calvary. Maybe his last gift, the most precious pearl in the world, could buy the life of the King. But as he rushed toward Golgotha, Artaban came upon a young girl running away from a band of soldiers. "Please help me," she cried. "My father is in debt and they are taking me to sell as a slave to pay what he owes! Please save me!" Artaban hesitated. Then, sadly, he took out the pearl, gave it to the soldiers, and bought the girl's freedom. Now his last gift for the King was gone!

Suddenly, there was an earthquake, and Artaban was critically injured by some flying debris. He sank half-conscious and dying to the ground. Then, like a whisper from very far away, there came a voice: "I assure you that when you have done it for one of the least of these brothers and sisters of mine, you have done it for me" (Matthew 25:40). And Artaban smiled, even as he died, because he knew the King had indeed received all his gifts.

Christmas gives us a new picture of God, and Christmas gives us a new understanding of others. As Artaban's tale shows, God very often stands before us in the other people we meet. When we

THE GIFT OF A NEW UNDERSTANDING

see them, when we help or refuse to help "the least of these," we help or refuse to help Jesus himself. Christmas serves as a reminder of that reality and gives us a new understanding of others. In other people, we see a reflection of God. With this new understanding, we come to know that the best way to serve God is to love God's children.

Christmas Gives Us a New Purpose for Living

Christmas gives us the gift of new understanding by providing a new sense of direction, a new meaning for our lives. This new purpose is to share in the Christmas story, to celebrate God's love daily and pass it on to others. When we do so, we dedicate everything we do to God. What higher purpose could there be than that?

Have you ever wondered why we put tinsel on our Christmas trees? There are several legends about the origin of tinsel, and many of them involve spiders in some form or another. One such legend tells of a spider who saved Jesus' life as Joseph, Mary, and their young child were fleeing to Egypt trying to escape from Herod's soldiers. William Barclay tells the story in *The New Daily Study Bible, Volume 1: The Gospel of Matthew* (Westminster John Knox Press, 2001), pages 40–41.

Joseph, Mary, and Jesus traveled all day, hurrying away from Bethlehem. Evening came and they were tired, so they sought refuge and warmth in a cave. It was very cold, so cold that the ground was white with frost. A little friendly spider saw the Christ Child and somehow wished that he might do something to help him or to keep him warm in the cold night. He decided to do the only thing he could: He spun a web across the entrance to the cave, to make a kind of curtain there in hopes that the web might keep some of the cold night air out of the cave.

Later that night, as some of Herod's soldiers were carrying out his order to kill the children of Bethlehem, they came to the cave. They were about to burst in to see if there was anyone hiding inside, but the captain noticed the spider's web, covered now with frost and stretching right across the entrance to the cave. The web was unbroken, he noticed, and he reasoned that there couldn't possibly be anyone inside the cave. Otherwise, the web would have been disturbed. The captain instructed his men to go on without searching the cave, confident that they would be wasting their time.

So the soldiers passed on by and left the holy family in peace, because a little spider had spun his web of love across the entrance to the cave. And that, so they say, is why to this day we put tinsel on our Christmas trees. The glittering tinsel streamers stand for the spider's web, white with frost, stretched across the entrance of the cave on the way to Egypt.

The spider had spun his web many times before, but this time it was with a new purpose. The spider's work this time was not to capture insects for food, but to provide warmth for the Son of God. When he encountered the Christ Child, the spider received a new understanding of his gifts—the ability to spin a web—and how he might use them in service of God. The spider's web was dedicated to God and as a result, it meant life!

This is our purpose for living, the new understanding of our lives and our world that Christmas gives to us. We are called to bring life rather than death, to bring love rather than hate.

Christmas gives to us the gift of a new understanding, which affects our relationship with God, our relationship with other people, and our relationship with ourselves. At Christmas, we receive a new picture of God, and it is a picture of love. At Christmas, we receive a new view of other people, in which we come to recognize God in them. And at Christmas, we receive a new perspective on our own life, in which we find that our purpose is to live for God.

I hope that you will claim this Christmas gift of a new understanding today.

Questions for Reflection and Discussion

1. Read Mary's song of praise (Luke 1:46-55) closely, and count all the instances of reversal that she proclaims (such as God lifting up the lowly and pulling down the powerful). How do these reversals point to a new understanding of the world in which we live?

2. How does Mary's song give you a new understanding of God? What aspects of God does she describe that are different from your usual expectations?

3. How has your understanding of God changed over the years? What have been the most important factors that gave rise to this change?

4. *What is your best understanding of God now? What would it mean for you to have a new understanding of God?*

5. *How does the message above challenge you to see other people differently? What would change in your life right now if you had a new understanding of others?*

6. *What drives you to get out of bed every morning, or what gives you a sense of joy and fulfillment? How might this become a part of God's larger purpose of life and salvation?*

Prayer

Lord God, you are the one who gives sight. Open our eyes to see you differently, to see our neighbors differently, and to have a fresh vision of our purpose in your world. Give to us this day a new understanding, so that we might see ourselves as you see us. Help us to know the height and depth of your love, so that we might rest in it and share it with all others. Amen.

Focus for the Week

This week, serve another person or people. Partner with your church or a local mission agency, or respond on your own to someone's need. Recognize the presence of God in others, and allow your new understanding to manifest itself in service and action on their behalf. Challenge yourself to make this the beginning of a regular habit of service and love.

Daily Devotions

Read the Scriptures for the daily devotions and reflect on what they say to you about the gift of a new understanding. Record your insights in the space provided, using the questions at the top of each page as a guide.

Day 1

1 Kings 3:4-15

A Prayer for Understanding

Solomon realized the value of understanding and wisdom. Given an opportunity to ask God for anything, the king prayed for "a discerning mind in order to govern your people and to distinguish good from evil" (1 Kings 3:9). God granted his request, giving to Solomon "a wise and understanding mind" as well as wealth and fame, things Solomon hadn't asked for (1 Kings 3:12-13). Scripture and tradition both continue to recognize Solomon for his great wisdom.

We long to have a good understanding of ourselves and of our world—to discern good from evil, and know how God desires for us to live. During Advent, we have an opportunity to embrace a new, true understanding as a gift from God. Christ invites us into a new way of seeing God, a new way of seeing others, and a new way of seeing ourselves. Blessed with this new understanding, we can follow Jesus with confidence and gratitude, striving to see the world and everything in it through God's eyes.

When have you prayed for understanding? How did God respond to your prayer?

How have you come to understand God, others, or yourself differently through the experience of Advent or Christmas, either this year or in years past?

Day 2

Romans 12:1-21

Transformed Minds, Transformed Relationships

"Don't be conformed to the patterns of this world, but be transformed by the renewing of your minds so that you can figure out what God's will is—what is good and pleasing and mature" (Romans 12:2). In Paul's vision of life in Christ, God's grace changes the way we think. No longer do we understand things in the familiar patterns of this world; our very minds are changed and we begin to see things in a new, God-centered way. We come to see ourselves differently, understanding our bodies as a living sacrifice to God and not thinking of ourselves too highly (Romans 12:1, 3). And we come to understand others differently, seeing everyone's gifts and recognizing our interdependence (Romans 12:4-8).

This renewal of our minds transforms our relationships. By God's grace, we are empowered to love without pretense, regarding one another as family, rejoicing with those who are happy and crying with those who are sad. We can repay good for evil. We can seek peace with all people, striving for relationships marked by equality and mutual love. All of these things stem from a renewed understanding, given by God, that changes how we see others and ourselves. What a tremendous gift!

How has God's grace transformed your mind, allowing you to see things differently than you have in the past?

How does a new understanding of others change your relationships with them? How is God seeking to change your mind right now?

Day 3

Luke 15:11-32

A Father's Joy

In the parable of the prodigal son, Jesus gives us a moving picture of God by telling of a father's dramatic, unexpected response to the return of his wayward son. The son in this familiar story has done everything wrong: He's requested his share of the family's inheritance while his father was still alive and then wasted it all on reckless living. He's been brought to the lowest point in his life, feeding pigs and longing to eat even the pigs' food because of his hunger and poverty. Eventually, he makes the difficult decision to return home and beg for a place as a servant in his father's house. Knowing he doesn't deserve to be treated as a son, the young man resolves to ask only to be a servant, hoping his father will give him this small kindness.

The father's surprising reaction tells us everything Jesus wishes to communicate about God. The reaction is one of overwhelming joy and love, nothing else. The father isn't angry, and he requires nothing of the son in order to earn back his status. He's simply happy that his son has returned—it's as if he's come back from the dead—and there is nothing to do but celebrate. Such is God's attitude toward us. When we go astray, God is eager to welcome us back and filled with joy when we return. God is full of love.

When have you been overwhelmed by God's love?

How has your understanding of God changed over the course of your life? How have you come to understand God's love for you?

Day 4

Luke 10:25-37

The Good Samaritan

"Who is my neighbor?" (Luke 10:29). A legal expert asked Jesus this question after he and Jesus had discussed the need to love God with all one's heart, soul, strength, and mind, and to love one's neighbor as oneself. Jesus answered this question with a parable. His response gave the man a new understanding of what *neighbor* could mean, causing him to see that it meant everybody.

Samaritans were considered outsiders for Jews, but in Jesus' parable a Samaritan showed kindness and righteousness by helping a man who had been beaten and left for dead by thieves. A priest and a Levite had both passed by the man without helping him, even though they saw him lying there. The Samaritan, then, is the one who behaved like a neighbor toward the injured man. In this story, Jesus reshapes our understanding of who our neighbors are. It's no longer about Jew versus Samaritan, us versus them, insider versus outsider. Instead, it's about who shows us mercy and those to whom we show mercy. Neighbor is defined by the breadth of our kindness and love, as well as the kindness and love shown toward us.

Have you ever received love and kindness from an unexpected source? How did you respond?

How does Jesus' parable challenge and inspire you to broaden your own kindness and love toward others?

Day 5
Exodus 31:1-11

Gifts and Abilities

"Look, I have chosen Bezalel, Uri's son and Hur's grandson from the tribe of Judah. I have filled him with the divine spirit, with skill, ability, and knowledge for every kind of work" (Exodus 31:2-3). God has delivered the Israelites from slavery in Egypt, and God is now giving Moses instructions for building the Tabernacle in the wilderness. The Tabernacle's construction will be good, holy work, and God has given Bezalel and others the skills and abilities to carry out the task. They will be the craftspeople who prepare the Tabernacle and other instruments of worship.

Back in Egypt, Bezalel and others likely used their skills in service to Pharaoh as part of the Israelites' slavery and heavy labor. Now, they get a new opportunity to use their abilities in service for God. They received a new vision of how their talents might be used for God's glory, and with it surely came a renewed sense of purpose and meaning. With the same skills, they could now labor with joy knowing that their work would provide vessels for God's presence in the Israelites' midst. When God sets us free, God sets us to work in ways that will bring glory to God and fulfillment within ourselves.

What skills and abilities do you use in service to God?

How might God be calling you to use your gifts in a new way for God's glory?

Day 6

1 Corinthians 12:1-11

Spiritual Gifts

"A demonstration of the Spirit is given to each person for the common good" (1 Corinthians 12:7). The Bible is clear that all who follow Christ receive the Holy Spirit, and Paul here affirms that the Spirit shows up differently in the life of each person. Though each person's gifts will be different, they are all given from the same Spirit. Moreover, these gifts are meant for the good of the whole Christian community, not just for the benefit of the ones who receive them.

Paul's words to the Corinthians are an invitation for us to look within and discover the gifts that the Holy Spirit is nurturing in us. How is the Spirit manifesting itself in your life, and how will this build up the people around you? The list of spiritual gifts Paul names in 1 Corinthians 12:8-10 shows us a range of possibilities, but it is not exhaustive. What Paul wants us to know is that these gifts all come from the same Spirit, so they are not in competition with one another, and they are meant as gifts for the whole community of faith.

What spiritual gifts do you have?

How are you using these gifts to build up your fellow Christians?

3. The Gift of a Strong Foundation

Joshua 24:14-15

Be Careful What You Lean Your Weight On

A number of years ago my wife, June, and I left our hometown in Memphis, Tennessee, and went up north to Ohio to live for three years. We were in our early 20s at the time, and we had been married for a year when we went up there so I could go to seminary. While I did my three years of theological school, June finished up her remaining three years of college. To say we were busy would be to put it mildly.

We were both going to school full-time and holding down four jobs between us to pay for school and put bread on the table. I was going to seminary, serving two churches, and working as a janitor on the seminary campus. June was going to college and working as the assistant librarian at the seminary, while she also worked as the assistant librarian at the Ohio State Observatory which was next door to the seminary campus.

During our second year up there in Ohio, Christmas fell on a Sunday, so we had to devise a Christmas plan. Here's what we came up with:

We'd finish all academic requirements, classes, projects, papers, and final exams by Friday, December 23.

We'd do all our Christmas shopping on Saturday, Christmas Eve.

We would celebrate Christmas Eve Communion at both of our churches on Saturday evening.

I would preach Christmas morning, and then we would get in our little Volkswagen Beetle with our Christmas purchases from the day before, and drive fourteen hours to Tennessee to celebrate Christmas with our families.

This meant that we had to do all of our Christmas shopping in one day. So early on that Christmas Eve Saturday morning, we went to the huge Lazarus department store in downtown Columbus, Ohio. When the doors opened at 10:00 A.M., we rushed into this big department store that spread over four city blocks, and we "covered" every inch of it that day. We didn't have much money, so we had to shop carefully. Finally, late that afternoon we were exhausted and I thought we were through. But, no. June thought of some more gifts we needed to care for . . . and she decided she would make them in the car the next day on the long drive home!

So, we went to the fabric department. Now, I can hang in there pretty well with the shopping when you are just buying ready-made gifts. But fabric shopping is not my cup of tea. I just go weak; all the strength in all of my muscles goes away, and my legs and arms begin to feel like wet spaghetti. So as June continued to shop for the fabrics she needed, I took the two completely filled shopping bags and started looking for a place to sit down. No luck! There was not an empty chair anywhere in sight. But, there were all of these large bolts of material on display throughout the fabric department. The department was filled with fabrics draped this way and that, which created a beautiful display.

I began to look for a bolt fabric I could lean against. Then I saw it . . . a large bolt of black material over toward the corner. It was a perfect resting place, the next best thing to a chair. There I was with those two large, heavy shopping bags (one in each arm), with clear instructions from June not to put them down. So, I went over and leaned back against that soft bolt of black material.

Oh, it was so wonderful! I was so tried and it felt so good to lean my weight on that bolt of black material. I was resting there so nicely, when all of a sudden I felt this strange sensation. I thought: "I'm so tired I'm just imagining things, but it felt like that bolt of material moved." And then I realized it did move! I turned around. That bolt of black material turned around . . . and I found myself looking into the sweet, angelic face of an elderly Roman Catholic nun.

I was so embarrassed. My face turned red as a beet, and I stammered out the only thing I could think of to say in that moment: "I'm sorry. I thought you were a bolt of material!" Oh, no. What a terrible thing to say! I couldn't believe I had said that. I tried to say some other things, all of which were wrong. Finally, I just blurted out: "I am so sorry." The elderly nun smiled, then she reached over and patted my cheek and said, "My son, your sins are forgiven . . . and you have made my day!" Then she winked at me and turned and walked away.

Now, the moral of that story can be summed up in a pun: "Those who look before they lean need not worry nun!"

But more seriously, that story raises a much-needed warning for us: "Be careful what you lean your weight on!" In other words, be careful where you put your trust. This warning is so fitting for us today, because everywhere we go there is an incessant clamoring for our trust, our allegiance, our energy, our resources, our commitment, and the weight of our influence. Everywhere we go, every step we take, someone is either screaming loudly or whispering temptingly in our ears.

> Put your trust in me!
> Put your hope in me!
> Give your allegiance to me!
> You can count on me!
> Lean your weight on me!

Money says that. Military might says that. Gangs and cliques say that. Alcohol and drugs say that. Material possessions say that. They all say enticingly, put your trust in me. Give me your allegiance. Hope in me. Lean your whole weight on me.

Now, this is precisely what this Scripture lesson in Joshua 24 is all about. Remember how forcefully Joshua said it:

> *But if it seems wrong in your opinion to serve the* Lord, *then choose today whom you will serve. Choose the gods whom your ancestors served beyond the Euphrates or the gods of the Amorites in whose land you live. But my family and I will serve the* Lord. *(Joshua 24:15)*

We will put our trust in the Lord. This is without question one of the greatest statements in the whole Bible. And it is a great verse to think about as we move toward Christmas because the hectic demands of Christmas these days can indeed pull us and push us in all directions. And all of these directions can indeed scream out for our time, our energy, and our allegiance, just as the gods beyond the Euphrates or the gods of the Amorites did for the people of Israel in Joshua's day.

"Choose today whom you will serve. . . . But my family and I will serve the Lord." What was the context of this strong statement of Joshua's allegiance? What prompted Joshua to say that? If you listen to those words closely, you can hear a lot of strong commitment in his word, but also a tone of exasperation. You see, after all those years of wandering in the wilderness, the Hebrews had now come into the Promised Land. They had dreamed of this. They had longed for this. They had prayed for this. But now that they were in the land, they had a new big problem: Other people lived in the land, too. These other people had their own set of gods they worshiped. They had household gods, gods of fertility, gods of storms, gods of this and that and the other. And some of these false gods looked attractive to the Hebrews, so much so that they were tempted to worship them instead of worshiping the Lord (which, of course, was a blatant violation of the first commandment).

Joshua saw what a danger this was, and so he gathered the Israelites together so that the people could recommit themselves to serving the Lord. First, Joshua reminded them of everything God had done for them, bringing their ancestor Abraham to Canaan and giving him offspring. Joshua reminded them how God brought them up out of slavery in Egypt, and of God's great victory at the Red Sea. Joshua reminded them how God had enabled them to conquer the people in Canaan, not through their own strength but through God's presence and might (Joshua 24:1-13). Then Joshua exhorted them to serve the Lord, who had done all these great things for them. Boldly, dramatically, strongly, he laid it on the line. He said: "But if it seems wrong in your opinion to serve the LORD, then choose today whom you will serve. Choose the gods whom your ancestors served beyond the Euphrates or the gods of the Amorites in whose land you live. But my family and I will serve the LORD" (Joshua 24:14-15).

A story from Joshua might be a strange one to read during Advent. But this story in Joshua is about choices, decisions, commitments, and priorities, all of which come into focus in the days and weeks leading up to Christmas. It's about deciding to whom we will give our allegiance, our loyalty, and our trust. The Israelites in Joshua's time were faced with a choice of which gods to worship. It's the same for us, though we don't think today of literal gods in control of the weather or our wars. Instead, our gods are things like money, or fame, or a bad crowd, or ambition. Will we lean our weight on these things and serve them as if they can support us? Or will we lean on something stronger?

The choice of what we will lean our weight on is one of the most crucial choices we can make. That's why this is such a great story to think about in the Advent season. In the days and weeks leading up to Christmas, many "other gods" come front and center. Is there any time of year when we are tempted more to think about our possessions? What about the fullness of our calendars? As we move toward Christmas, we have to make a crucial decision. Will I put my trust in these things, or one of the many others that clamor for it? Or will I put my trust in something else? To whom or to what will I give my allegiance? Where will I place my hope? Where will I lean my weight this year? What will be for me a strong foundation?

Now, let me say three things about that and give you three recommendations for a strong foundation that you can discover this Advent and Christmas.

The Strong Foundation of Family

Joshua said, "My family and I" (Joshua 24:15), or, in another translation, "as for me and my household" (NRSV). Family was obviously a priority for him. Family should likewise be a priority for us, especially at Christmas. To underscore how important this is, remember that two of the Ten Commandments call for loyalty to the family. Commandment number five tells us to honor our parents (Exodus 20:12), and commandment number seven tells us to be faithful in marriage (Exodus 20:14). In doing so, they both remind us that strong families produce a strong nation, and weak families produce a weak nation.

Oh, how we in the modern world need to hear afresh these commandments. Family life is breaking down all around us, and it is tearing our society apart. Drug abuse, homelessness, sexual promiscuity, violence, abuse, public profanity, emotional illness, crime, and other social problems are strangling the very life out of our world. Many of them are caused, or at least made worse, by the breakdown of family life in our time. I wonder how many people who find themselves in these or similar situations would tell you that their problems are rooted in a bad situation at home, a destructive or abusive family life.

Put that over against this: Some years ago, our church and our city took a blow to the heart. One of our best, Randy Smith, had a massive heart attack and died. Randy, so full of life, so full of faith, so full of joy, was suddenly gone. I still have trouble believing it sometimes. The next morning, I sat down with Randy's family to reminisce about Randy; I spoke at length with Ann (his wife of more than fifty years), and the children, Randy Jr., Meg, and David.

We cried together, laughed together, and prayed together as we remembered "Randy stories." At one point I said to the children, "When you think of your dad, what jumps immediately into your mind. Here's what they said:

His way of always seeing the good

His joy of life

His sense of humor

His commitment to Christ

His love of the Bible

His love for the church

His service in the community

His love for our mom

His unconditional love for us

Then they expressed what I would call three "quotable quotes." They said,

"His love for us children was the perfect example of God's love."

"He treated a federal judge and the parking lot attendant exactly the same."

"He was the perfect example of what a Christian should be."

Now, think of that. Wouldn't that be something, to come to the end of your days on this earth and have your family remember you like that? It doesn't get any better than that. I was so touched by that experience because it reminded me again that the home is where we receive our first instructions in the virtues, our first lessons in right and wrong, our first brush with unconditional love, our first call to faithfulness. Randy and his wife cultivated a strong family, and this family was his foundation to be a good man in the world. And for his family, Randy served as a strong foundation that they could lean upon.

The importance of family shows up in the Christmas story as well. Genealogies in Matthew 1:1-17 and Luke 3:23-38 show Jesus' connection to his family, and it's easy to imagine how Joseph and Mary would have been there for one another through the strange and difficult circumstances of Mary's pregnancy and Jesus' birth. And for many people today, Christmas is a time to celebrate with family, even when it is difficult.

One of the great lessons of Christmas is the reminder of how important the family is. And that's what we need to lean our weight on: not on the latest passing fad, but on the enduring values of the Christian family.

The Strong Foundation of the Church

Joshua speaks of his family and their commitment to serve the Lord, but it's important to remember his audience when he says this. Joshua is addressing the whole people of Israel, the whole community of God's people. He speaks for the commitment of his family, but he challenges everyone to make the same commitment. He wants for them to reject the other gods, as he has done, and serve the Lord alone. He wants all of them, not just his family, to live faithfully. Joshua's challenge shows the importance of the whole community of faith. That community of the Israelites could be for each individual a strong foundation. Translated into today's terms, we can say that the church is a strong foundation.

I deliberately put these thoughts in this order (the church right beside the family) for this reason: We all know that some children and young people and, indeed, some adults are not getting what they need at home. It's sad but true. If that's the case for you, then come to the church. Turn to the church. Let us be your family. Let us give you the love and the discipline and the supervision and the support you need.

I know a young man who had a tough situation at home. His father had deserted the family. They had not heard from the father for years. This young man's mom was doing the best she could, but to make ends meet, she had to work two minimum-wage jobs. One was during the day and one was at night, and consequently, she was never home. So that young man adopted the church as his family, and we adopted him. We became his family. He just pretty much lived at the church. He chose to lean his weight on the church, and now he is one of the finest young men I know. For this young man, the church was a strong foundation, and it was a wonderful, life-changing gift.

Advent and Christmas draw the church together like no other season of the year. Christmas plays bring children and families to the church for celebrations. Advent Bible studies bring people together for learning and fellowship. Holiday service opportunities bring the church together in service of neighbor. And Christmas worship services are some of the most heavily attended services of the year. Christmas is a reminder of the strong foundation of the church in our individual lives and in our communities.

Be careful where you put your trust. Be careful where you put your hope and confidence. Be careful what you lean your weight on, and choose only a strong foundation. Christmas underscores dramatically and beautifully how important it is to lean your weight on the strong foundations of your family and your church.

The Strong Foundation of God

Joshua shows the importance of his family when he says "my family and I" (Joshua 24:15), and he recognizes the importance of the whole community of God's people when he addresses the Israelite nation. But his whole reason for speaking is to exhort and challenge the people to serve the Lord alone. For Joshua, God is the strongest foundation possible. Serving other gods is like leaning upon a weak, shifting foundation that is unable to support you. But because God has done great things for the people—calling Abraham, delivering them from slavery in Egypt, and conquering their enemies in the Promised Land—God has proved to be a firm, strong foundation for the people's trust, faith, and love.

That's what faith is, after all. It is trusting God, come what may. It's committing your life to God and leaning your weight on God in every circumstance. That is what Joshua meant by calling the Israelites to serve the Lord alone. And that is precisely what Mary and Joseph did at the first Christmas. They didn't understand all that was going on, but they trusted God and followed God's lead. They did their best and trusted God for the rest. They leaned their weight on God, and God was a strong foundation.

And that is what we are called to do!

A little girl had somehow received a bad cut in the soft flesh of her eyelid. The doctor knew that some stitches were needed, but he also knew that because of the location of the cut, he should not use an anesthetic. He talked with the little girl and he told her what he must do. He asked her if she thought she could stand the touch of the needle without jumping. She thought for a moment and then said, "I think I can if Daddy will hold me while you do it." So the father took his little girl in his lap, steadied her head against his shoulder and held her tightly in his arms. The surgeon then quickly did his work and sewed up the cut in her eyelid. All the while the little girl did not flinch. She just held on tight to her father.

That's a parable for us in our spiritual lives, and a graphic reminder that whatever we have to face, we can hold on tight to our Father. We can trust God and count on God and lean on God. We can lean our whole weight on God's everlasting arms, which will be a strong foundation for us just as it was for Mary and Joseph on that first Christmas, and just as it was for Joshua and the Israelites many centuries before. God is our foundation.

What a wonderful Christmas gift!

Questions for Reflection and Discussion

1. What are the alternatives that Joshua sets before the Israelites in Joshua 24:14-15? Why were they tempted to worship the other gods Joshua mentions?

2. According to Joshua 24:1-13, what reasons do the Israelites have for worshiping the Lord alone? How do their past experiences shape their present and future expectations?

3. Think of a time in the past when you have leaned your weight on a weak foundation. What was the result of that experience, and what did you learn from it?

ALL I WANT FOR CHRISTMAS

4. *Name some things that clamor for your trust or loyalty in the time leading up to Christmas. How can you ensure that you only put your ultimate trust in the things that can truly support you?*

5. *If someone were looking at your behavior, what might they identify as the foundations that you build your life upon? Be honest with yourself about where you put your time, your energy, your attention, and your trust. How does your answer to this question challenge you or encourage you?*

6. *Based on Joshua 24:14-15 and the reflection above, what relationship do you see between family, the church, and God?*

Prayer

Lord Jesus, we know that you are our firm foundation. Thank you for being the solid rock that we can lean upon and depend upon, and thank you for the gifts of church and family by which you support us. Give us grace and trust to lean our weight on you, and give us the wisdom and the discipline to stay away from weak foundations. Help us to live our lives trusting in your faithfulness, at Christmas and always. Amen.

Focus for the Week

Choose one of the foundations above that need strengthening in your life: your family, your church, or your awareness God's presence. This week, spend some focused time and energy working on those foundations. Spend some time with your family, or tell them how much you appreciate them. Serve at church in a new way, or spend some extra quiet time with God this week. As you work to strengthen this foundation, ask how you can place more trust in this area of your life rather than on something less.

Daily Devotions

Read the Scriptures for the daily devotions and reflect on what they say to you about the gift of a strong foundation. Record your insights in the space provided, using the questions at the top of each page as a guide.

Day 1
Joshua 24:1-13

What God Has Done

Before Joshua challenges the Israelites to "choose today whom you will serve" (Joshua 24:15), he exhorts them to serve the LORD because of all that God has done for the people. In Joshua 24:1-13, Joshua reminds the people of their history, how God brought them into being and sustained them at every moment. From God's call of Abraham through the return to the Promised Land, God has been with them. The Israelites have received deliverance, protection, and victory in battle. And "it wasn't [their] sword or bow that did this"— it was their God (Joshua 24:12). They knew they could trust and serve the LORD, because God had done so much for them already.

In the same way, our past experience of God's grace forms the basis for our own trust and commitment to God in the present and future. We know that God is a strong foundation, because God has been there for us before. In the words of Joshua: "So now, revere the LORD" (Joshua 24:14). Because the Lord has done great things for us!

How have you experienced God's grace in the past, and how does that ground your commitment to God now?

What other events in the Bible and in Christian history would you add to Joshua's list of the great things God has done for God's people?

Day 2
Matthew 7:24-27

A House on Bedrock

At the end of the Sermon on the Mount, Jesus compares a wise builder to a foolish one. The wise builder sets his house on a strong foundation of bedrock, while the foolish builder constructs his house upon sand. What sets the builders apart is the foundation that they choose to build upon.

There are many, many things that we could choose to build our lives upon. We can make lives based upon money, or popularity, or possessions, or comfort, or pleasure, or power, or any number of other things. But all of these foundations are as shifting and unsteady as sand upon the beach. Lives built upon them will fall, just as the house upon sand fell when the storm came through. But we have another option: We can choose to build our lives upon the words of Jesus Christ, hearing them and obeying them. Lives built upon that foundation will be as strong and unshakable as a house built upon bedrock, capable of withstanding any storm.

When have you been shaken because you placed your trust in a weak foundation?

What words of Jesus are hardest to hear and obey? What do you stand to gain by obeying them anyway?

Day 3

Matthew 1:1-17

The Family Tree

The Gospel of Matthew, the first book in the New Testament, opens with a genealogy of Jesus, tracing the Messiah's ancestry all the way back to Abraham. This says something about the relationship between the Old Testament and the New Testament, namely that the two are deeply connected. The birth of Jesus is the next chapter in the long story of Abraham's family.

We see some of the highlights of this story in Matthew's genealogy, reminding us of the hopes and dreams that Jesus brings to fruition. The mention of Abraham, Isaac, and Jacob (Matthew 1:2) shows us that God's promise to Israel's ancestors finds fulfillment in the descendant who would be a blessing to his people and the whole world. The mention of David the king (Matthew 1:6) reminds us that Jesus is the long-awaited Messiah, the anointed royal descendant who would rule God's people with righteousness and justice. And the mention of outsiders such as Rahab (Matthew 1:5) shows us that God's love expressed in Jesus extends to all people. The New Testament begins by recounting Jesus' family tree. The life, death, and resurrection of Jesus are built upon the foundation of the story of God's people in the Old Testament.

*What connections do you find between the Old Testament and the
New Testament? How do these shape your understanding of Jesus?*

How does your past serve as a foundation for your current experience of God?

Day 4

Matthew 18:15-35

Where Two or Three Are Gathered

"Where two or three are gathered in my name, I'm there with them" (Matthew 18:20). The church is a strong foundation, because we experience Jesus' presence through common life with other believers. This is not always as easy or uplifting as we might expect or prefer. Humans are imperfect; people will fall short. Relationships, even among followers of Jesus, can become strained. Jesus recognizes this, giving instructions on how to treat someone who sins. In the first part of the passage, he tells how to correct someone who sins gently but firmly, enlisting the help of more people if needed (Matthew 18:15-20). In the second part of the passage, Jesus lifts up the importance of forgiveness, telling a parable about an unforgiving servant to make his point clear (Matthew 18:21-35).

In our life together as Christians, we must balance gentle but firm correction with forgiveness and grace. Forgiveness does not mean allowing sin to continue. Correction does not mean holding a grudge or doling out punishment. By maintaining a balance between these, we bear one another up and strengthen one another in Christ.

When have you felt the tension between forgiveness and correction in a relationship with another person? How did you resolve it?

How do you experience Christ's presence when you are gathered with other Christians in Jesus' name?

Day 5

Genesis 15:1-6

Trusting God

"Don't be afraid, Abram. I am your protector. Your reward will be very great" (Genesis 15:1). In Genesis 15 God speaks to Abram, whose name will later be changed to Abraham, assuring him of God's protection and generosity. God has watched over Abram in times of danger, and God promises to provide him with a great reward. Abram, however, recognizes a potential obstacle to God's promise: He has no offspring, meaning that everything he receives from God will pass to another person upon his death. In response, God assures Abram that he will have a biological child, then promises him that Abram's offspring will number as many as the stars in the sky (Genesis 15:4-5).

God has already promised to make Abram a great nation (Genesis 12:2). Here, God does little more than reiterate that earlier promise. God offers no actual proof that Abram will have biological children, only a dramatic illustration of how many his promised offspring will number. Nevertheless, Abram trusts the Lord (Genesis 15:6). Abram has faith, and the promise is enough to assure him. Abram recognizes that God is a sure foundation, worthy of trust even when things seem difficult or impossible.

When have you trusted in God's promise despite not having proof?

How is God a trustworthy foundation for you?

Day 6

Matthew 11:2-6

Evidence of a Strong Foundation

When John the Baptist is in prison, he starts to wonder if Jesus truly is the Messiah that he and his fellow Jews have been expecting. Perhaps it is his experience of imprisonment that causes doubt to creep in, or perhaps Jesus is acting differently from how John thought the Messiah would act. Whatever the reason, John sends messengers to ask Jesus directly: "Are you the one who is to come, or should we look for another?" (Matthew 11:3). In response, Jesus points to his ministry, inviting John's disciples to report what they hear and see. Blind people are able to see; lame persons are walking; lepers are cleansed; deaf people hear; the dead are raised; the poor hear good news (Matthew 11:5).

John can trust that Jesus is the one to come because of the ministry of healing and reconciliation that Jesus brings about. In the same way, we can trust that Jesus is God's Son because of the healing and restoration he brings about in our lives and in the lives of others.

What works of healing has Jesus brought about in your life or the life of someone close to you?

How do you know from "what you hear and see" that Jesus is the Messiah, the Son of God?

4. The Gift of a New Style of Living
Matthew 23:23-26

Christianity Is Not Just a Creed We Profess; It's a Lifestyle We Live

Let me tell you about a very special Christmas present I received some years ago from our granddaughter, Sarah. Sarah was seven years old at the time, and the gift was a beautiful tie. It had a black background with all kinds of sports objects on it: footballs, baseballs, basketballs, soccer balls, volleyballs, tennis rackets, ice skates, and running shoes. That same Christmas, she gave June a beautiful necklace. It has a gorgeous cross made of pearls hanging from a gold chain.

Now, these gifts are special to us not only because they are from our granddaughter Sarah, but also because of the way she selected and bought them. Her elementary school had a gift shop, which was run by the older elementary children. The gift shop was set up to teach the students how to shop—how to make their own choices, using their own money. The parents did not come with them. The children came to the gift shop on their own, selected their gifts, and paid for them out of their own pockets. Sarah went to the shop and bought the cross necklace for June and the sports tie for me. And of course, we love them.

When we thanked Sarah for our gifts and complimented her on her excellent choices, she said, "Well, Gran, I know you love sports." When June asked her why she picked the necklace with the cross on it for her, she said, "Mimi, I know you go to church a whole lot!"

I know this sounds like a proud grandfather talking, but Sarah did have a unique knack for saying the most interesting things.

Before she was two years old she came up with a name for our church. She labeled it "Jesus' Castle." She could always (so often) come up with just the right words for the moment.

It's a great feeling when you are able to do that, to come up with the exact right words for a given situation. Unfortunately, most of us know all too well the flip side of that coin: those awful, agonizing moments when we are at a complete loss for words. Or even worse, those moments when we inadvertently blurt out the wrong thing and are reduced to an embarrassing, shameful silence. This has happened to me many times.

For example, I once complimented a woman on her beautiful maternity dress. To which she replied coldly and venomously, "For your information, this is *not* a maternity dress!" Now let me ask you, what do you say to that? I didn't know what on earth to say. I couldn't even stammer out an apology. I was reduced to an embarrassing silence.

That's the way it goes. Sometimes we are at a complete loss for words, and those moments are awkward, sometimes painfully so. But the real truth is that most of the time most of us do pretty well with words. We are fairly eloquent. We talk a pretty good game. Our real problem, it turns out, is with actions. We lack the ability to follow through on the words we speak. We talk too much and do too little. We verbalize so well and actualize so poorly. We speak so eloquently and perform so inadequately. We spout high-sounding words into the air, and then we put acting off until tomorrow. But we must surely know that "talking a good game" is not enough. Only when our words are translated into actions are they authenticated. Only then do they make a difference.

Nowhere is this truer than with matters of faith. It's not enough to preach our faith from our pulpits. It's not enough to sing it in our hymns. It's not enough to talk about it in our Sunday school classes. Faith is a lifestyle. It's a whole new way of living!

This is what Paul meant when he wrote these words: "Live together in a manner worthy of Christ's gospel" (Philippians 1:27).

In other words, let your conduct, your behavior, your actions, your everyday routine, your tone of voice, and every other aspect of your life be worthy of Christ. Paul is right on the mark here because Christianity is not merely a set of intellectual ideas. It is not merely a collection of theological beliefs. It is not merely a series of philosophical arguments. It is a way of life, a way of acting and responding, a way of relating to God and to people. It's a lifestyle . . . and it's a lifestyle that works! The gift of Christmas is an invitation to embrace this new lifestyle, to take on this new way of living and recommit ourselves to it.

Christianity is not just a way of believing; it is also a way of behaving. That's what Jesus is talking about in Matthew 23 when he chastises the Pharisees and legal experts who neglect the most important matters of the law even as they rigidly perform others (Matthew 23:23-26). Our faith is not just something we proclaim and celebrate in the sanctuary one day per week, and it's not just something that we can perform step-by-step with no effect on our real selves. It is something we live out and demonstrate and share with others at home, in the office, on the street, on the tennis court, or on a date. It's a matter of heart and life.

I once ran across a story about something that happened in Africa some years ago which makes the point well. Some missionaries wanted to go into a remote corner of Africa to set up a Christian mission station to work with a tribe of people who lived there. The missionaries didn't know how they would be received, so as a sign of good will they flew over in an airplane and dropped by parachute a bright, shiny new plow as a gift to the African tribe. A few days later, the missionaries came in expecting that their gift would have made the tribe more receptive to them. But instead, they found something they hadn't counted on. The people of that tribe had never seen a plow before. They didn't know what this strange looking instrument was or why it had dropped from the skies. And so, not knowing what else to do with it, they had put the plow up on a pedestal and they were worshiping it.

That plow, of course, was designed to be used, not revered. It was designed to strike deep into the African soil and make it easier to obtain food for their tables. It was designed to work for the people, to help the people, to nourish the people, to make them healthier, to make their quality of life better. But because the members of the tribe didn't know that, they made the plow an ornament rather than a tool!

Something like this is what we are always tempted to do with our faith: to make it an ornament rather than a tool. So often, we think of our faith as an object of veneration rather than a means to personal and social transformation. So often, we see it as a lovely set of ideals to be laid neatly upon a pedestal rather than as a powerful force designed to revolutionize our manner of life, and indeed, the whole fabric of society. This, again, is the message Jesus brought home to the legal experts and Pharisees who tithed mint, dill, and cumin but neglected to pursue justice, peace, or faith (Matthew 23:23). With their actions they worshiped their religious belief rather than truly using it for the good for which it was intended.

This was what so upset the eighth-century prophets. This is why Amos, Micah, Hosea, and Isaiah got so angry with the people of their time. This is why these great prophets cried out so dramatically. They felt (and rightly so) that unless your religion changes your life, it is a farce. Unless your faith touches your moral behavior, it is just so much hypocritical play-acting. Liturgies, ceremonies, and holy feasts were good if they helped produce righteous lives. But if they did not produce this good fruit, they were a stench in the nostrils of God.

This is strong imagery, but it's what the prophets said. They spoke out for God and they said, "I hate your feasts. I despise your ceremonies. I want love, truth, kindness and righteousness, and not sacrifices and burnt offerings." The point is clear: Talking (or believing) a good game is simply not enough. The point is that unless creeds are translated into deeds, they become dull, insipid, dead, worthless. If our faith is not lived out, if we don't practice what we preach, if our Christian profession doesn't burst forth into Christian expression, then it is, to quote Shakespeare, only "sound and fury, signifying nothing."

Let me break this down a bit further. Only when we live our faith does it become compelling, contagious, and convincing. Look with me quickly at those three Cs one at a time.

Only When We Live Our Faith Does It Become Compelling

When our words and our beliefs are translated into action, only then do they really take hold of our lives. John Mott, longtime leader of the YMCA and recipient of the Nobel Peace Prize, once decided to try to really discover the meaning and power of prayer. He attended lectures on prayer. He listened to sermons on prayer. He researched the biblical references to prayer. He read everything he could get his hands on about prayer. But he came up empty. Then, at some point, he discovered the answer. He started praying! He made prayer an active part of his life. He had read more than seventy books on prayer, he realized, but only when he actually started praying did prayer become a real, powerful, compelling force in his life!

That's the way it works. We can recite our creeds, and we should. We can study our Scriptures, and we should. We can research our doctrines, and we should. But only when our faith is translated into action, only when our beliefs take root in our daily living, only then is our religion worth its salt, only then is our Christianity compelling and powerful in our own lives and in the world around us.

Only When We Live Our Faith Does It Become Contagious

Doctrines, creeds, ideas, and beliefs—no matter how true, no matter how eloquent, no matter how perfectly phrased—carry very little conviction in themselves. It is when they walk before us in flesh and blood that they become contagious. As author George Eliot once put it: "Ideas are often poor ghosts. Our sun-filled eyes cannot discern them. But sometimes, they are made flesh. They breathe upon us with warm breath. They are clothed in a living soul. Then their presence is a power!"

That's how it is with Christian faith. The truths of our religion are most impressive, most inspiring, most influential when they are wrapped up in living persons. God knows that. That's why God sent Jesus into the world on that first Christmas: So we could see the truth wrapped up in a person.

The most effective argument for Christianity is a real Christian. The supreme argument for our holy faith is a holy life. Daniel Webster once said that the best argument he knew for Christianity was an old aunt of his who lived up in the New Hampshire hills. The truth is that the people out there on the street are not that interested in our theologies, or our liturgies, or our vestments. The people out there are pragmatists. They don't want to know the history of our faith, or the intricate theological details that undergird our beliefs. What they want to know is, "Does this thing work?" They are tremendously interested in that.

When he was pastor of Riverside Church in New York, Dr. Harry Emerson Fosdick gave an illustration that makes the point dramatically. He told of how, during the course of the Armenian Genocide in the early 1900's, a young Armenian woman saw a Turkish soldier brutally kill her brother. He had chased them down the street into a dead-end alley. While the soldier was finishing the killing of her brother, the young woman escaped. Later, she was captured, and since she was a nurse, she was put to work in a military hospital where she was forced to bring healing to the enemy. Then one day, ironically, the soldier who had murdered her brother was brought into the hospital and placed in her ward under her care. He was critically wounded and she was his nurse. Their eyes met. They recognized each other immediately. Terror flashed into his eyes. He was so seriously injured that the slightest inattention would cause his death. The nurse struggled within. One part of her cried, "Vengeance . . . here is your chance . . . no one will ever know." But the Spirit of Christ within her won out, and she conscientiously nursed him tenderly back to health. Each day she cared for him. Each evening she prayed for him.

Later, the soldier asked her, "Why? You recognized me. Why did you care for me so faithfully, so diligently? You had the perfect chance to get me back. Why didn't you?" She said, "Because I serve Him who said, 'Love your enemies and do them good.' That is my faith." After a quiet moment, the Turkish soldier said, "Tell me more of your religion. Tell me more of your Lord. I would give anything to have a faith like yours."

The woman embraced a new, Christian style of living by extending forgiveness and showing compassion to her enemy. And as a result, her enemy came to desire this Christian way of life for himself as well. When our faith is lived out, only then does it really become compelling and contagious.

Only When We Live Our Faith Does It Become Convincing

When we truly live out our faith, it becomes not only compelling, but convincing. People believe it because they see its effect in our own lives, and they can't deny that it's real. Norman Neaves, who served for many years as pastor of The Church of the Servant in Oklahoma City, once told a wonderful story that speaks to this. Several years ago, a teacher assigned to tutor children in a large city hospital was asked to help a particular young boy with his schoolwork. The boy had been seriously burned in an accident. The boy's regular teacher told the tutor that they were studying irregular verbs and dangling participles. She was concerned that without help during his extended hospital stay that he might fall too far behind. So the visiting teacher went to the hospital to work with that youngster. But when she got there, she was horrified to discover that the boy was in the Critical Care Unit . . . and that he had been burned so badly all over his body that he could barely talk.

Nevertheless, dedicated teacher that she was, she tried her best to work with him on his irregular verbs and dangling participles. When the teacher left, she felt a bit distraught and honestly didn't know whether she had helped him or not. But the next morning, when the tutor came back, the head nurse was all smiles. She said, "You worked a miracle yesterday! We have been so worried about him. He had been so depressed and so unresponsive. He had given up. He wasn't trying to get well. He was just lying there waiting to die. But ever since you came, his attitude has changed. He is talking; he is working with us. He is fighting back, and he's beginning to respond to treatment. We believe he is going to make it. He is going to live after all!"

The teacher was pleased, but dumbfounded. She had no idea what she had done at all. Some weeks later, after the boy had been released from the hospital, he explained why the teacher's visit had made such a difference. It was a simple realization that had come to him that night after the teacher had left. He said, "They told me I would live, but I didn't believe them. I thought they were just humoring me. I thought they were just saying that I would live. But then when you came, it made all the difference. I realized that they wouldn't send a teacher to work with a dying boy on irregular verbs and dangling participles!"

They had told him he would live, but it didn't convince him. They had reassured him, but it didn't convince him. Their words were simply not enough. But the action of that teacher coming to help him with his homework made all the difference. In her actions, he saw undeniable proof that he was expected to live, and he believed it himself.

Here again we see it. Actions speak louder than words. They are more compelling, more contagious, and more convincing.

How can your actions at Christmas this year bear witness— a true, powerful witness—to the faith that you confess and believe, that the very Son of God was born in Bethlehem to save us? How can your actions at Christmas this year compel and convince someone of the power of God's love, so that it becomes contagious? How can you wash the inside of the cup—your own heart and life— and truly live out your faith? What difference would that make?

Questions for Reflection and Discussion

1. Take a close look at Jesus' words in Matthew 23:23-26. What shortcoming does he see in the actions of the Pharisees and legal experts?

2. How would you describe the true, good way of life that Jesus envisions based on what he tells the Pharisees and legal experts?

3. Think of a person you know who truly seems to live out his or her faith, making it a matter of his or her whole heart and life. What is it about this person that gives you this impression?

4. In what ways do you find this person's faith to be compelling, contagious, or convincing?

5. Name some of the key characteristics of a Christian way of life. What practices, attitudes, or thought patterns set this way of life apart from all others?

6. How do Advent and Christmas call our attention to this distinctive lifestyle? What opportunities does it hold for us to embrace this way of life with a new commitment and energy?

Prayer

Loving God, we know that we are wary to accept the gift of a new lifestyle that you offer to us this Christmas. We see it before us and recognize it in others and in your Scriptures, but we so often fail to live it out ourselves. Help us. Give us courage and grace to live out our faith even when it is difficult. Let our faith manifest itself in our actions and in our attitudes, so that our very lives bear witness to the trust we have in you. Amen.

Focus for the Week

This week, focus on one attitude within that needs to change if you are to receive the Christmas gift of a new style of living. Perhaps you are quick to judge others, or slow to forgive; perhaps you love your friends well enough, but the same love doesn't extend to strangers or enemies. Whatever it may be, commit yourself to a new attitude throughout this week. Let this be the first step into a new way of life that is compelling, contagious, and convincing!

Daily Devotions

Read the Scriptures for the daily devotions and reflect on what they say to you about the gift of a new style of living. Record your insights in the space provided, using the questions at the top of each page as a guide.

Day 1

Philippians 2:1-11

Imitate Christ

"Adopt the attitude that was in Christ Jesus" (Philippians 2:5). Exhorting his readers to seek the welfare of others rather than their own good, Paul lifts up Jesus as an example to imitate. Christ Jesus was "in the form of God" (Philippians 2:6), but chose to empty himself, becoming like a human being and being obedient even to the point of death on a cross (Philippians 2:7-8). For Paul, Jesus exemplifies a new style of living, one characterized by humble obedience rather than ambition or self-promotion. Paul encourages this same style of living among the Philippians, instructing them to watch out for others rather than for themselves (Philippians 2:4).

The words Paul uses to describe Christ Jesus in Philippians 2:6-11 are a hymn-like confession that the Philippians already knew. Paul recalls it here to remind them of the new lifestyle they are to adopt. Our confession of Christ forms the basis for the new way of living to which we are called. We know who Christ is from our Scriptures, creeds, and Christian tradition. We are called to imitate him and pursue a life of humble obedience, putting our confession of Christ into practice in the way that we live.

Where does your knowledge of Christ come from?

How do you "adopt the attitude that was in Christ Jesus" in the way that you live every day? What can you do to accomplish this more fully?

Day 2

Luke 3:7-14

Change Your Heart and Life

John the Baptist called for repentance, a change of heart and life among his hearers. The forerunner of Jesus, John baptized people as a sign that they wanted God to forgive their sins (Luke 3:3). But John preached a harsh message showing that baptism alone wasn't enough. "Produce fruit that shows you have changed your hearts and lives," John says (Luke 3:8). In other words, don't just ask for forgiveness. Truly change your attitude and behavior. It's not enough to be a descendant of Abraham; one must produce the fruit of a good, faithful life.

John gave specific instructions about this type of life to those who came to be baptized. Those who had plenty must share with those who did not. Soldiers and tax collectors should do their work justly and with integrity (Luke 3:11-14). Those who followed these instructions and adopted a changed way of life could look forward with hopeful expectation to the coming of the Christ. The good news that John proclaimed was a call to respond. This remains true today. The good news of Jesus Christ challenges us to respond with a changed way of life. How will you respond?

How have you responded to the good news of Jesus Christ?

What fruit do you need to produce as a result of your changed heart and life?

Day 3

Galatians 5:16-25

The Fruit of the Spirit

In this passage, Paul contrasts actions driven by selfish desire with actions produced by the Spirit. The two are in opposition to one another; to be guided by the Spirit is to reject selfish impulses. Paul lists the types of actions produced by selfish desire (Galatians 5:19-21) as well as the behavior that is the fruit of the Holy Spirit (Galatians 5:22-23). Neither of these is a comprehensive list, but both are meant to give a clear picture of the two different lifestyles. Christ has set us free, but freedom must not become an opportunity to indulge selfish desires (Galatians 5:13). Paul encourages his readers to follow the Spirit, living in a way that causes the latter list of qualities and characteristics to emerge within us.

Most strikingly, Paul seems to say that we cannot always trust our own desires: "You shouldn't do whatever you want to do" (Galatians 5:17). Rather, those who belong to Christ "have crucified the self with its passions and desires" (Galatians 5:24). Living by the Spirit, Paul implies, is not easy. It requires a struggle within oneself. But the good news is, those who undertake this struggle are guided by the Spirit and belong to Christ Jesus.

What else would you add to the list of actions produced by selfish desire (Galatians 5:19-21) and the list of the fruit of the Spirit (5:22-23)? Why?

How do you struggle inwardly to live by the Spirit as Paul describes?

Day 4

Exodus 20:1-17

The Ten Commandments

"I am the LORD your God who brought you out of Egypt, out of the house of slavery" (Exodus 20:1). The well-known list of Ten Commandments stands at the beginning of laws that God gives to the Israelites at Mount Sinai. God has just brought them out of Egypt, setting them free from bondage to Pharaoh and the heavy labor it entailed. Now, God gives them instructions for living as God's people, laws that will undergird their relationships with God and with one another.

When God sets us free, God does not just send us on our merry way. God replaces one way of life with another. God frees the Hebrews from slavery to Pharaoh so that they might serve God in worship and love. The laws God gives to the people of Israel aren't meant to be restrictive, but are a gift to guide them into fullness of life with God and with one another. In the same way, God frees us from sin so that we might love God and neighbor. The life to which we are called as Christ's followers is a gift, not a burden.

What significance do the Ten Commandments have for Christians today?

What things do you do, or avoid doing, because you are a Christian? How does doing or avoiding these things lead you into a better relationship with God or with others?

Day 5

John 13:31-35

Love Each Other

After Jesus predicts his betrayal at the Last Supper, he tells the disciples, "Where I'm going, you can't come" (John 13:33). Immediately after this, Jesus gives the disciples a new commandment: "Love each other" (John 13:34). Jesus has loved his disciples, and they must love one another in the same way. Moreover, their love for one another will be the way everyone else will identify them as Jesus' disciples. They will be known by love.

Love each other. Those are Jesus' parting instructions, knowing that where he is about to go his disciples will not be able to follow right away. If Christmas gives to us a new style of living, Jesus' words here show that love is the most important aspect of this lifestyle. We won't be known by our faith, or by our miraculous signs, or by our righteousness, but by our love. This new commandment will guide our lives until we too are able to join Jesus in the Father's house.

THE GIFT OF A NEW STYLE OF LIVING

How is your lifestyle characterized by love?

How does love help others to see Christ in you and in your church?

Day 6

John 1:1-18

The Word Became Flesh

"The Word became flesh and made his home among us" (John 1:14). John's Gospel opens with a poem about the Word. This is John's Christmas story, describing the preexistent Word of God and how the Word came down to be among humans. The Word is identified with God, and is associated with life and light. All creation came into being through the Word.

We might wonder at the powerful, poetic nature of John's description of the Word. But we marvel all the more at the claim John makes in verse 14: "The Word became flesh and made his home among us. We have seen his glory." This supernatural Word of God, source of life, light, and being, became flesh and came to be with humans. That is the miracle we anticipate during Advent, the impossible event we celebrate at Christmas: the Word becoming flesh, the infinite becoming finite, God becoming human. As you turn your attention toward Christmas, recognize the truly miraculous nature of what we celebrate, and do not let it pass by unnoticed. God is with us!

What does it mean that the infinite, all-powerful Creator of the universe came to make his home among us?

How does this recognition shape your understanding of Christmas and what it means?

5. Christmas Gifts We Can Pass on to Others

Matthew 2:1-12

Christmas Gifts That Always Fit

Over the last several weeks, we have discovered some truly wonderful gifts that Christmas has for us. But the story of the wise men coming to Jesus reminds us of the Christmas gifts we can pass on to others. That is, after all, the origin for our practice of giving gifts at Christmas. Remembering their witness and following their example of giving precious gifts to Jesus, we celebrate Christmas by giving gifts to others. In the spirit of this book, I want to ask about the truly special, priceless, and timeless gifts that we can give. What are the true gifts of Christmas that we can pass on to others?

There is another way to think of these gifts, the gifts we can pass on that are not physical or tangible but are still very real. One year, I was really getting into the Christmas spirit of it all as I finished up my gift-giving preparations. I was right there with Santa, even "making a list and checking it twice." Just then, I discovered that I needed another kind of list. I needed a list of sizes. A size list is very important because we want our gifts to others to fit. But then, as I was working on my gift list, my mind drifted away from the practical task at hand and I found myself thinking deeper thoughts. I started to think about Christmas gifts that always fit and are always appropriate. The Christmas gifts that always fit . . . what would they be? If you made a list like that, what would be on it? As you think about that (if you'll pardon the pun), let me ask you to try these on for size.

The Gift of Time

The gift of time is a Christmas gift that always fits, and it's one that we can pass on to others. In the busy, frantic, hectic pace of Christmas, it may well be that the most precious and most valuable gift we can give someone we love is a little slice of time. A little uninterrupted time just for someone else is often priceless.

"The greatest gift I ever received," said a respected and successful attorney, "was a gift I got one Christmas when my Dad gave me a small box. Inside was a note which read: 'Son, this year I will give you 365 hours, an hour a day every day after dinner. It's yours. We'll talk about what you want to talk about. We'll go where you want to go. Or we'll play what you want to play. It will be *your* hour. This is my gift to you this year, the gift of *time!*'

"My dad not only kept the promise of that gift," the attorney said, "but that time together became so special to us that he renewed it every year and it's the greatest Christmas gift I ever received in my life."

This raises an interesting question we might want to consider this year at Christmas: "Is there someone near you to whom you need to give a little time?" Perhaps you are a college student coming home for the holidays, wondering what to give your parents. What could be better than just a little slice of time, time just for them? Or perhaps you are a high school student out of school for a few days, but still very, very busy with shopping and dates and Christmas programs and parties. Wouldn't it be nice to give just a little bit of time to your folks, or to your grandparents or other relatives? Or maybe you are a professional with vacation days to manage, travel to book, gifts to buy, and other holiday busyness crowding your already busy schedule. What better gift could you give to those closest to you—friends, coworkers, or relatives—than a little bit of undivided time, of undistracted attention just to spend with them? Or maybe you are a parent rushing to and fro, here, there and everywhere, coping with long lines and traffic jams, and heavy schedules, pouring over checklists of things to be done, decorations to be arranged, trips to be planned, food to be cooked, gifts to be selected, toys to be bought, cards to be mailed, presents to be delivered, bills to be paid. Wouldn't it be great in the midst of all that chaos and confusion, to find a little uninterrupted and unhurried time for your children? So many people need the gift of time. Husbands, wives, grandparents, shut-ins, people who are sick or lonely or in grief: Maybe the best thing to give them in this sacred season is a little time. The gift of time is always appropriate, and we can always pass it on. The gift of time always fits.

The Gift of Kindness

Christmas is that time of year when our emotions are taxed a bit and it is easy to become impatient and irritable. We often feel so much stress and anxiety that we take it out on others and treat them with less grace than we like to admit. But it doesn't have to be that way. We don't have to be thoughtless, or rude, or edgy, or harsh, or hostile. We can be kind! I think that one of the most impressive emblems of Christian faith is kindness. You can be an authority in theology, you can speak of the great philosophers, you can master church history, you can quote verses of Scripture. But only when I see your kindness, only then, do I really begin to see your faith.

It's a bit like Paul's words on love in 1 Corinthians 13:

> [1]*If I speak in tongues of human beings and of angels but I don't have love, I'm a clanging gong or a clashing cymbal.* [2]*If I have the gift of prophecy and I know all the mysteries and everything else, and if I have such complete faith that I can move mountains but I don't have love, I'm nothing.* [3]*If I give away everything that I have and hand over my own body to feel good about what I've done but I don't have love, I receive no benefit whatsoever.*

The same, I think, can be said of kindness. If we have all sorts of knowledge, even profound gifts such as prophecy or leadership skills, but lack kindness, our faith is severely limited. Kindness and grace toward other people is a basic expression of our love and trust in God, evidence of the Holy Spirit working in our hearts.

For those who receive it, the gift of kindness can be powerful. Such a gift can take many forms: a helpful or hopeful word for someone who needs to be lifted up; or a gentle reply to someone who is rude; or an honest effort to listen when someone has a complaint; or an unexpected gesture of goodwill to a stranger. Whenever or however it is received, the gift of kindness always fits.

Is there someone near you who, this Christmas, more than anything else, needs the gift of kindness?

The Gift of Appreciation

We don't have to be thoughtless. We don't have to take people or things for granted. I am convinced that people are hungry for appreciation, and because of that it is a Christmas gift that always fits.

Some years ago, when Dr. William L. Stidger was at the Boston School of Theology, he sat down one day to write some notes of appreciation to people who had touched his life in special ways and had influenced him for good over the years. He remembered a favorite schoolteacher, a woman who had taught him English in secondary school. She had gone out of her way to help him. She had kindled in him a burning hunger for knowledge. She had inspired him and taught him how to write. She had put deep down in him a love for literature. She had influenced his life and the lives of countless other students greatly. And so, years later, William Stidger sat down and scribbled off a quick note to his former teacher to say "thanks."

A few days later, he received this reply:

> My dear Willie, I cannot tell you how much your note meant to me. I am in my eighties now, living alone in a small room, cooking my own meals, lonely (and, like the last leaf of autumn), lingering behind.

You will be interested to know that I taught school for
fifty years, and yours is the first note of appreciation I
ever received. It came on a blue-cold morning and it
cheered me as nothing has in many years.

When Dr. Stidger read that note from his former teacher, he cried.
Stidger thought of other people who had been kind to him. He
remembered one of his bishops who had been most helpful to him
at the beginning of his ministry. The bishop was in retirement and
had recently lost his wife. William Stidger sat down and wrote a
belated letter of thanks to this former bishop. Back came this reply:

My dear Will, your letter was so beautiful, so real,
that as I sat reading it in my study, tears fell from my
eyes, tears of gratitude. Then before I realized what I
was doing, I rose from my chair and called my wife's
name to show it to her—forgetting for a moment
that she was gone. You will never know how much
your letter has warmed my spirit. I have been
walking about in the glow of it all day long.

The gift of appreciation may be the most fitting gift you and I could
give someone this Christmas. Stop and think for a moment about
all the people who have been there for you in ways large and small.
Have you let them know what they have meant? Can you pass on to
them the gift of appreciation?

The Gift of Encouragement

There is a wonderful verse in the Book of Isaiah where the prophet
announces that the Lord has given to him "an educated tongue to
know how to respond to the weary with a word that will awaken
them in the morning" (Isaiah 50:4). Wouldn't it be great if all of us
had the ability to encourage people when they are down, when they
are tired, when they are low? Over the last few days I have been

reading and enjoying Bill Lufburrow's book entitled *Illustrations Without Sermons* (Abingdon Press, 1985). Bill Lufburrow, a good friend, was president of Goodwill Industries of Houston, and he taught the Goodwill Class at St. Luke's United Methodist Church when I was pastor there. In his book, Bill tells of an interesting experience he had in Houston one Christmas.

It was 9:45 in the evening. The front door bell rang. When Bill opened the door, he found six or eight children, ranging in ages from six to ten, standing there. Their spokesman said proudly: "Hi: We're cheering up the neighborhood." Then he counted, "one-two-three," and they all yelled loudly: "Cheer! Cheer! Cheer!!!" And with that, the children disappeared as quickly as they had arrived.

Isn't that great? Little children spreading cheer, little children cheering up the neighborhood, little children being the sons and daughters of encouragement. On a silent and holy night a long time ago, encouragement came to the world as never before, through a little child. When you really think of it, you want to pass on the gift of cheer, cheer, cheer! So what better gift could we give someone this Christmas than the gift of encouragement? It's a gift that is always appropriate. It's a gift that always fits.

The Gift of Love

Finally, of course, the most important gift of all is the gift of love. Love truly is what it's all about. What the people near us need this Christmas season, more than anything else, is the gift of love.

In the early 1500's, the great Protestant reformer Martin Luther was preaching a sermon on the Christmas story. Luther asked his congregation to meditate on the events surrounding the birth of Jesus as if it were their story. Rather vividly, he pictured Mary: tired, cold, afraid, so young, and having to be both mother and midwife during her labor. And he pictured Joseph, nervously trying to help as best he could.

All of a sudden, Luther turned on his congregation. He had anticipated their reaction, and he said to them that he knew what they were thinking. He told them they were thinking: "If only I had been there. How quick I would have been to help with the baby. I would have washed the linen. How happy I would have been to go with the shepherds to see the Christ Child, or bring a gift to the manger with the wise men." Luther went on to tell them that they would have served during the birth of Jesus in such ways because they knew how great Jesus is. But if they had been there at the time, without knowing Jesus, they probably would have been no better than the people of Bethlehem. "Childish and silly thoughts are these," Luther said. "Why don't you do it now? You have Christ in your neighbor, so why don't you serve your neighbor now? For what you do to your neighbor, you do to the Lord Jesus Christ himself."

The message is clear: When we love others, we do nothing less than loving Jesus himself. We should not fool ourselves into thinking that we love Jesus any more than we love those around us. And we should not forget that we truly love Jesus when we love our neighbors. As the hymn-writer so aptly put it: "Love Came Down At Christmas." What could be more fitting than to receive that love and then to pass it on?

Time, kindness, appreciation, encouragement, and love. These are a few Christmas gifts that always fit. I'm sure you will think of other ones. These are the Christmas gifts that we can pass on to others. And the good news of Christmas is this: In giving these wonderful gifts to others, we give them to Jesus himself. We, too, can give to Jesus a gift every bit as precious as what the wise men brought. When we give the gift of time to someone in need, we are spending time with Jesus. When we give the gift of kindness to another person, we treat Jesus with kindness. When we show appreciation toward someone else, we give Jesus the gift of appreciation. When we encourage someone who is weary, we encourage Jesus himself. And when we love another person, we give to Jesus the gift of love.

Of all the gifts we want from Christmas—good news, new understanding, a strong foundation, or a new lifestyle—the greatest one is the gift of Jesus Christ himself, the embodiment of God's love and grace coming to be with us. And that is a gift we can pass on to others by sharing Christ's love with them.

Questions for Reflection and Discussion

1. Read Matthew 2:9-11 about the gifts that the wise men brought to Jesus. What do these gifts symbolize? How well do they "fit" based on who Jesus is?

2. How do you think Mary and Joseph responded to these gifts, and to the wise men who showed up at their door?

3. Think about the "Christmas gifts that always fit" from the reflection above. Which of these gifts, if any, did the wise men give to Jesus? How does their journey to present gifts of gold, frankincense, and myrrh point to these precious, timeless gifts?

4. When have you received the gift of time, kindness, appreciation, encouragement, or love from another person? How did you respond to it? How valuable was it?

5. Which of these gifts is the hardest for you to give to someone else? Why?

6. The reflection above reminds us that when we love others, we love Jesus as well. How would Jesus respond to the gifts that you give to others, if you were giving these gifts to Jesus directly? How does your answer affirm or challenge your practice of gift giving at Christmas?

7. *How can you pass on the Christmas gift of time, kindness, appreciation, encouragement, or love to others this year?*

Prayer

Lord Jesus, we thank you for these precious Christmas gifts of good news, a new understanding, a strong foundation, and a new way of living. Give us the grace to recognize these gifts and claim them for our own, not just at Christmas but throughout our lives. We know that we meet you in other people. Guide us and transform us as we pass on valuable gifts of time, kindness, encouragement, and appreciation to others. And above all, help us to remember always that the greatest gift is love. Amen.

Focus for the Week

Identify one of the gifts above: time, kindness, encouragement, appreciation, or love. Which of these gifts is God calling you to give? Think of one person to whom you can pass along this gift this week. Perhaps you can spend an hour or two of time with someone who is lonely, or perhaps you can give someone a phone call to express your gratitude and appreciation. After you decide, give this person your "gift that always fits" this week.

Bonus: Organize a Churchwide Advent Study

*A*ll I Want for Christmas: Opening the Gifts of God's Grace leads readers to discover the gifts that Christmas has for us, and how we can experience those gifts through the miracle of God's presence in Jesus Christ. In addition to this book and the accompanying video and Leader Guide, resources for youth and children are also available to facilitate a churchwide, intergenerational program.

Such a program provides opportunities for Christians of all ages to learn from one another, worship together, and celebrate the season of Advent through a shared experience.

Resources for the Churchwide Study

Adults

All I Want for Christmas: Opening the Gifts of God's Grace, by James W. Moore
All I Want for Christmas: Opening the Gifts of God's Grace Leader Guide, by John Gilbert
All I Want for Christmas: Opening the Gifts of God's Grace DVD

Youth

All I Want for Christmas: Opening the Gifts of God's Grace: An Advent Study for Youth, by Cindy Klick

Children

All I Want for Christmas: Opening the Gifts of God's Grace Children's Leader Guide, by Suzann Wade

Sample Schedule

Many churches have weeknight programs that include an evening meal followed by separate classes for children, youth, and adults. The following schedule provides one suggestion for organizing a weeknight program based on *All I Want for Christmas: Opening the Gifts of God's Grace.*

5:30 P.M.	Meal
6:00 P.M.	Intergenerational gathering introducing Bible passages and main ideas for the lesson. This time may include skits, music, and prayers.
6:30-7:45 P.M.	Classes for children, youth, and adults.

Churches may want to do the Advent study as a Sunday school program rather than a weeknight program. While this would be similar to a weeknight setting, the suggested schedule does not include a meal and meeting times are shortened to fit a normal Sunday school schedule.

10 minutes	Intergenerational gathering
45 minutes	Classes for children, youth, and adults

Churches may also choose to do the Advent study as a weekend retreat. This setting includes meals, worship, intergenerational gathering times, and classes for children, youth, and adults. The suggested schedule below allows for teaching of all the content in a condensed two-day time frame.

Friday

5:30-6:00 P.M.	Light dinner
6:00-6:30 P.M.	Worship
6:30-8:00 P.M.	Session 1 classes for children, youth, and adults

Saturday

8:30-9:30 A.M.	Worship
9:30-11:00 A.M.	Session 2 classes for children, youth, and adults
11:00-11:30 A.M.	Intergenerational gathering
11:30am-12:30 P.M.	Lunch
12:30-2:00 P.M.	Session 3 classes for children, youth, and adults
2:00-2:30 P.M.	Intergenerational gathering
2:30-4:00 P.M.	Session 4 classes for children, youth, and adults
4:00-5:30 P.M.	Session 5 classes for children, youth, and adults
5:30-6:00 P.M.	Closing worship

Choose a schedule that works best for your congregation and its existing Christian education programs. Adapt the suggested schedules above to fit your needs.

See the Leader Guide, Children's Study, and Youth Study for ideas about how to make the most of your intergenerational gathering time, with prayers and suggested activities that everyone can do together.

Everything you need to turn this book into
an all-church Advent study

Help your whole church explore the wisdom in popular author James W. Moore's *All I Want for Christmas*. The complete selection of resources is listed below. 5 sessions.

9781501824197. Adult Study Book
9781501824210. Adult Study Book Large Print
9781501824203. Adult Study eBook
9781501824227. Leader Guide
9781501824234. Leader Guide eBook
9781501824241. DVD
9781501824258. Youth Study Book
9781501824265. Youth Study eBook
9781501824272. Children's Leader Guide

Visit your local book retailer for details.

AllIWant_ND_RegPrint5in5x8in5

CPSIA information can be obtained
at www.ICGtesting.com
Printed in the USA
FSHW021222061218
54268FS

9 781501 824197